A Note to Parents

READERS is a compelling program for be~~g~~ █████████████████
conjunction with leading literacy experts, i. **W9-BCW-917**
Emerita Distinguished Professor of Education at Clemson University.

The ReaderActives line provides action-oriented images, colorful page designs, and stories in which children get to make their own choices. Multiple story paths encourage children to reread their adventures to explore every possible ending. Each ReaderActive is guaranteed to capture a child's interest while developing his or her reading skills, general knowledge, and love of reading.

Unlike traditional READERS, ReaderActives are not assigned a specific reading level. Generally, ReaderActives are best suited to Levels 2 and 3 in the list below. Younger children will surely enjoy making the story's choices while adults read aloud to them. Likewise, older children will appreciate picking their own path and trying new options with each reading.

Pre-level 1: Learning to read

Level 1: Beginning to read

Level 2: Beginning to read alone

Level 3: Reading alone

Level 4: Proficient readers

The "normal" age at which a child begins to read can be anywhere from three to eight years old. Adult participation through the lower levels is very helpful for providing encouragement, discussing storylines, and sounding out unfamiliar words. No matter which ReaderActive title you select, you can be sure that you are helping your child learn to read interactively!

Prima Games Staff

VP
Mike Degler

Licensing
Paul Giacomotto

Marketing Manager
Jeff Barton

Digital Publisher
Julie Asbury

Credits

Publishing Manager
Tim Cox

Creative Services
Wil Cruz

Production
Beth Guzman

The Prima Games logo and Primagames.com are registered trademarks of Penguin Random House LLC, registered in the United States. Prima Games is an imprint of DK, a division of Penguin Random House LLC, New York.

DK/Prima Games, a division of Penguin Random House LLC
6081 East 82nd Street, Suite #400
Indianapolis, IN 46250

ISBN: 978-0-7440-1948-3 (Paperback)

ISBN: 978-0-7440-1952-0 (Hardback)

Printing Code: The rightmost double-digit number is the year of the book's printing; the rightmost single-digit number is the number of the book's printing. For example, 18-1 shows that the first printing of the book occurred in 2018.

21 20 19 18   4 3 2 1

01-311221-Nov/2018

Printed and bound by Lake Book.

Alolan Academy

Written by Simcha Whitehill

HOW TO USE THIS READERACTIVE

Welcome to this Pokémon ReaderActive, where *you* decide how the story unfolds! As you read, you'll find instructions near the bottom of some pages of the story. These instructions fall into a couple of categories:

1. Some instructions tell you to skip to a certain page-they look this this:

> Continue to **PAGE 31** and choose your first Pokémon!

When you see an instruction like this, simply turn to the page that's listed and continue reading.

2. Other instructions let you make a choice. This is how you decide where the story takes you! Each of your options is described in its own bar, like this:

> If you want Oshawott to make a big blast and ride the wave out, go to **PAGE 10**.

> If you want Oshawott to fill the hole gently like a pool and swim its way out, go to **PAGE 42**.

Whichever option you choose, just skip to the listed page and continue reading. In the example above, let's say you decide to choose the first option. In this case, just turn to **PAGE 10**.

That's all there is to it! Don't forget-when you finish one story, you can start over, make different choices, and create a whole new adventure! Now it's time to head to school!

"Rrrrrrrriiiiing!" your alarm clock sings.

You open your eyes to see the sunlight sparkling through your window. The day is so bright you think you might get a suntan if you stay in bed. But that won't happen because today is the day you've been waiting all summer for— the first day at The Pokémon School!

Your new school is located in one of the most scenic spots on Melemele Island. From your classroom, you'll see why Alola is known for its natural wonders. There is a lush forest that leads to the entrance, a river that runs through the yard, tall trees that grow high above the bell tower, mountains rise in the distance, and the ocean shore creeps right up to campus.

You take a shower. Brush your teeth. Comb your hair. Put on the clothes you laid out last night. You eat a delicious Pecha Berry breakfast. You look at your watch—you got ready in a flash! You're excited to get to school early. This will give you extra time to set up your desk and make new friends.

Go to **PAGE 6**.

You walk over the footbridge and through the tall arch at the entrance to the Pokémon School. But you don't see any students. It sure is quiet. You check your watch again. You're early, but not that early. Where is everyone?

A woman walks by pushing a wheelbarrow full of dirt. She must be on the maintenance crew.

"Hello," you wave.

"Hiya!" she says back. "What are you doing here so early?"

"Oh, I'm a new student," you explain. "So, I wanted to be early."

"Welcome to the Pokémon School!" she replies. "But I'm sorry to tell you, you're a whole day early. Class doesn't start until tomorrow."

Your jaw drops on the floor. School doesn't start for a whole other day?! You can't believe you got the date wrong.

"I guess I should be going then," you say with a frown.

"If you want, you can hang out here in the yard," she offers. "Or go see Professor Kukui. He'll be your teacher and I bet he could use an extra pair of hands today."

To stay and play in the yard, go to **PAGE 43**.

To find Professor Kukui, go to **PAGE 7**.

You head to your future classroom to see if your soon-to-be teacher is there. You walk around the hallways looking at the beautiful view of the blue ocean and tree-covered mountains. You arrive at your classroom and knock on the door.

"Come on in!" you hear Professor Kukui say.

You introduce yourself as his new student. You explain that you accidentally got your days mixed up. Since you're already here, perhaps Professor Kukui could use your help.

"Well, today my plan was to find something special for one of my lessons. Want to come along?" Professor Kukui asks.

"That would be awesome!" you reply.

To trek to the mountains, continue below.

To hit the beach, go to **PAGE 19**.

Professor Kukui points at a giant green mountain in the sky.

"That's where we're headed," he says.

You can't wait to get there! First you have to cross the forest.

To travel on Ride Tauros up the mountain, go to **PAGE 8**.

To hike up the mountain, go to **PAGE 16**.

As you hike up the mountain path lined with so many lush trees, you see wild Pokémon! Before your very eyes, an Oricorio Baile Style sips the nectar of a bright yellow flower and turns into Oricorio Pom-Pom Style.

"Awesome!" you cheer.

You're so excited to get the chance to see Pokémon in their natural habitat! But one Pokémon isn't particularly happy to see you—Alolan Marowak.

It jumps right in front of you, swinging its bone. It's ready to battle. Is it Alolan Marowak's nature to always pick a fight? This is the first time you've met one.

"That's strange," Professor Kukui says, spotting a black bandana on the ground nearby. "This belongs to Team Skull."

Alolan Marowak is getting angrier by the second. You have to act—and act fast!

To have Crabrawler fight Alolan Marowak, continue to **PAGE 9**.

Or, to explain that you didn't come to the mountain to harm it, go to **PAGE 11**.

ORICORIO BAILE STYLE:
Dancing Pokémon

HEIGHT	2'00"
WEIGHT	7.5 lbs
TYPE	Fire-Flying

ORICORIO POM-POM STYLE

HEIGHT	2'00"
WEIGHT	7.5 lbs
TYPE	Electric-Flying

ALOLAN MAROWAK:
Bone Keeper Pokémon

HEIGHT	3'03"
WEIGHT	75.0 lbs
TYPE	Fire-Ghost

"Crabrawler, I need your help!" you say, tossing your Poké Ball.

Crabrawler comes out with its pincers swinging. This Fighting-type Pokémon is always ready for a battle!

"Crabrawler, use Crabhammer!" you ask.

Crabrawler's pincers are ready to slam, but Alolan Marowak cuts it off with its bone baton. Then it blows a Will-O-Wisp blaze right into Crabrawler's face.

"Hang in there, buddy," you say. "Try Dynamic Punch."

Crabrawler goes to swing, but Alolan Marowak blocks the Attack with its bone. It strikes again with back-to-back Bone Rush hits.

With one more mighty strike, Crabrawler foams at the mouth and faints. It is unable to battle.

"Thank you, Crabrawler," you say while returning it to its Poké Ball. "I'm going to take you to Nurse Joy for a nice rest. I'm sorry Professor Kukui, I wish I could help more."

"Don't worry, I can take it from here," he says.

You start down the mountain and wonder what Pokémon he's going to use to battle Alolan Marowak. But when you look back to check, you don't see any fighting.

"I am Professor Kukui. I am here from the Pokémon School," he says, pointing across Melemele Island to his classroom.

CRABRAWLER:
Boxing Pokémon

HEIGHT	2'00"
WEIGHT	15.4 lbs
TYPE	Fighting

"Alolan Marowak, that was an amazing battle. How do you feel? Can I take you to the Pokémon Center to rest?" Professor Kukui asks with concern.

Alolan Marowak shakes its head, but it is touched by the offer. It steps aside and extends its arm, offering Professor Kukui passage.

You can't believe it! That's all it took to get by Alolan Marowak?! Now you wish you had tried showing Alolan Marowak your heart because you have so much of it!

Professor Kukui knew just what to say. It looks like you just learned your first lesson from your new teacher. There will be plenty more time for lessons when school officially starts tomorrow.

THE END

"Marowak," you begin. "I am a new student at the Pokémon School and I am here to help my teacher, Professor Kukui, find a fossil. We mean no harm."

Professor Kukui holds up Team Skull's black handkerchief and asks, "Did Team Skull give you trouble?"

Alolan Marowak hangs its head. You hear a whimper nearby. It's another Marowak Alola form and it's injured. These two Alolan Marowak must have gotten into a very heated battle with the evil Team Skull.

"I'm Professor Kukui. Please, I'd like to help you. Can I give you some medicine and bandages?" he offers.

Alolan Marowak nods with gratitude. Professor Kukui covers the scratches on its ailing arm with a soothing medicine.

Next, the Alolan Marowak at the pass signals you to follow it.

You and Professor Kukui hike with Alolan Marowak up the pass to a break in the rock face. It leads you into a dark cavern. You can see where it is going by the green flames on its bone, but you take out your flashlight to watch your step. Soon, it stops and points to the ground.

You shine your light on a slab of rock with a wispy imprint.

"Amazing!" Professor Kukui cheers. "It's a fossilized feather from an ancient Pokémon. What an incredible find!"

"I can't wait to get this back to the lab and analyze it with Principal Oak. Thank you, Marowak!" Professor Kukui says.

"While you head back to school, I can take Marowak to Nurse Joy to rest," you offer.

Professor Kukui likes your plan and thanks you for being such a caring Trainer.

You and Alolan Marowak stand in the lobby of the local Pokémon Center.

"Marowak is going to be just fine," Nurse Joy promises.

You and Alolan Marowak take a seat and wait for your buddy to feel better. But why sit in a waiting room when you can be outside playing? It jumps up and twirls its bone as if to ask you to a battle.

"Count me in!" you say.

To call on Cranidos, continue below.

To choose Rowlet, turn to **PAGE 14**.

"Cranidos, I choose you!" you shout, tossing your Poké Ball.

Cranidos arrives on the field ready for a fun battle. Before Alolan Marowak can make a move, you ask Cranidos to charge at it with Head Smash.

You were hoping Marowak wouldn't see this move coming, but it's Cranidos that doesn't see what's next. Alolan Marowak aims a clever, close-range Bonemerang—its bone whacks Cranidos right in the back.

CRANIDOS:
Head Butt Pokémon

HEIGHT	2'11"
WEIGHT	69.4 lbs
TYPE	Rock

"Cranidos, are you okay?" you say.

"Crrrrranidos!" it says, bravely standing back up.

"All right, use Zen Headbutt!" you instruct.

Cranidos focuses all of its power to its mind. But its attack gets interrupted again by the repeated strike of Marowak's Bone Rush. Cranidos can't continue battling.

"Well done, Cranidos. You deserve a good rest!" you tell your pal. "Luckily, we're already here at the Pokémon Center."

"See you back in the waiting room!" you say, carrying Cranidos in to see Nurse Joy.

What an action-packed day you had! Now you think both you and Cranidos could use a rest before you start school tomorrow.

THE END

"Rowlet, I choose you!" you cheer, tossing your Poké Ball.

"Rrrrrr," Rowlet coos, confused as to why it was woken up from its daytime slumber.

ROWLET:
Grass Quill Pokémon

HEIGHT	1'00"
WEIGHT	3.3 lbs
TYPE	Grass-Flying

"Marowak!" the Alolan Marowak replies, seeing if Rowlet is ready for battle time.

The Grass Quill Pokémon stands up. It looks like the match is on! Marowak tries to surprise Rowlet with a perfectly aimed Bonemerang.

Rowlet sees the flaming bone coming and dodges it by flying straight up into the air.

"Awesome, Rowlet!" you say, encouraging your pal. "Now, send a Leafage storm!"

Rowlet releases an intense tornado of leaves that swirls around Marowak. While it's trapped, you have Rowlet swoop in with Brave Bird.

"Rrrrrrrr!" Rowlet yelps.

Then it slams into Alolan Marowak. With that powerful hit, Alolan Marowak is left unable to battle.

You toss a Poké Ball hoping to catch it.... Continue below.

The Poké Ball flashes as it rolls back and forth. ou watch it with so much excitement you don't even blink.

Bing!

You have caught your new Pokémon pal Alolan Marowak.

"Rrrrrr!" Rowlet cheers.

Now you both can't wait to start school with one more friend in tow.

THE END

TAUROS:
Wild Bull Pokémon

HEIGHT	4'07"
WEIGHT	194.9 lbs
TYPE	Normal

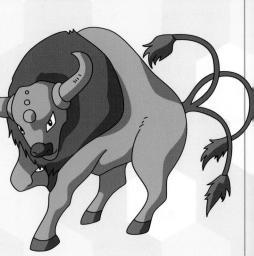

Two Ride Tauros snort as Professor Kukui leads them over.

"Hop on!" Professor Kukui says when Ride Tauros stops at your side.

Professor Kukui offers you a hand as you jump onto Tauros. Professor Kukui gets on the other Ride Tauros. Before you know it, you're galloping off into the forest.

"Yippee!" you cheer, enjoying the ride.

In no time, you're near the mountain and a fork in the road. it's time to make a decision.

The path to the left leads to the lush, green valley. The path to the right leads to rocky terrain with a big boulder. To go left, continue on the next page.

To go right, turn to **PAGE 18**.

As you get close to the mountain, Professor Kukui suggests you both hop off. This way you can keep your eyes peeled for unusual fossils.

"This valley is so full of greenery, I wonder if we can find a fossil of some prehistoric plants," Professor Kukui hopes.

You spot a jagged rock at the bottom of a bush. It has some kind of notch on it... Could this be a sign of ancient life? When you try to inspect it, you realize the rock is buried half under ground. You begin to dig.

You pull out the rock and dust it off with your hand.

"Look at that!" you cheer, alerting Professor Kukui. "I think I've found one!"

"Remarkable!" Professor Kukui says. "What a well-preserved fossil of a large ancient leaf. I can't wait to bring this back to school and do some research on prehistoric plants of the region."

Professor Kukui thanks you for all the help.

"Thank you for taking me along on this cool field trip," you reply.

After just one unofficial day of school, you just might say it is the best school ever!

THE END

Ride Tauros carefully steps from rock to rock. It's a bumpy ride, so you hold on tight.

"Hold it there, Tauros," Professor Kukui says.

He hops off and kneels down on the ground. He runs his hand over the cool grey stone.

"Hm, from the look of these stones, I'm guessing this land used to be covered in water," he says.

MAGIKARP: Fish Pokémon

HEIGHT	2'11"
WEIGHT	22.0 lbs
TYPE	Water

"Interesting!" Professor Kukui says, handing you the small stone. "This looks like a fossil of a Water type. Which one do you think it is?"

"I think it's a fossil of Magikarp," you say.

"I'm looking forward to having such a bright, adventurous, student in my class," Professor Kukui says.

"Well, I'll be there again tomorrow," you say with a chuckle.

THE END

You and Professor Kukui set out for the shore. It's a surprisingly short trip. You could see the ocean from your classroom, but you didn't realize just how close it really was.

Professor Kukui presents your mission, "We're looking for a fossil or something ancient from Alola, something that would show our awesome history," he says.

Now it's time to find it!

To dig around the rocky cliff, continue below.
To choose Beldum and use its magnetic pull, turn to **PAGE 29**.

Professor Kukui hands you a small red shovel.

"Ready to dig?" Professor Kukui asks.

"You bet!" you reply.

You pick a sunny spot a few paces away. You kneel down in the sand and toss the sand over your shoulder. You wipe the sweat off your face. You hope to find something soon.

"Huh!" you groan, putting your all into it.

Whap! You hit a rock and accidentally split your shovel in half.

To go grab a nearby abandoned shovel, proceed to **PAGE 25**.

Or, to hop onto a Ride Sharpedo and take it out on the water, go to **PAGE 20**.

Ride Sharpedo is so much fun! But it's swimming so fast, it's hard to search for treasure or fossils.

SHARPEDO:
Brutal Pokémon

HEIGHT	5'11"
WEIGHT	195.8 lbs
TYPE	Water-Dark

To have Sharpedo drop you off on the rocks so you can get a better look on foot, continue below.

To turn around and search the area with the help of Beldum, turn to **PAGE 29**.

You hop off Ride Sharpedo.

"Sharpedo!" it roars goodbye, leaving you standing on a rock in the middle of the ocean.

You suddenly realize it might be hard to get back to shore. But you push that thought out of your head.

You spot a slab with a marking.

"Wow!" you say, running your fingers over the stone. "That looks like a bone. I wonder where it's from?"

You can't wait to show Professor Kukui! Now you have to find your way back to shore with it.

The slab is nearly half your size and very heavy. You'll need some help to get it back to shore.

To signal for help from Alolan Raichu, continue below

To ask Rowlet to fly over to Ride Sharpedo, go to **PAGE 22**.

"Raichu, I need your help!" you say, tossing your Poké Ball.

It hops on its tail like a surfboard and catches a wave back to shore.

In no time, you spot Professor Kukui and Alolan Raichu coming toward you on Ride Lapras.

"Over here!" you shout, waving your arms in the air.

"I'm so glad you're okay! I was looking all over for you," Professor Kukui says. "How'd you get all the way out here?"

You explain what happened and apologize for not telling him where you went.

ALOLAN RAICHU:
Mouse Pokémon

HEIGHT	2'04"
WEIGHT	46.3 lbs
TYPE	Electric-Psychic

"But look, I found a cool fossil!" you say with a smile.

"Whoa! That looks like a bone from Gyarados. I'm glad you found it in fossil form, otherwise you would have been in real trouble out here by yourself," Professor Kukui warns.

"It is fun to explore Alola together, but alone it can be dangerous. That's why we always use a buddy system at the Pokémon School."

As you sail back to the beach, you promise Professor Kukui you'll never wander off again. He's right. Alola is more fun when you have pals to share it with. You can't wait to start school with a classroom full of friends tomorrow!

THE END

You toss your Poké Ball and Rowlet arrives asleep. It thinks daytime is for naps and nighttime is for play, but you need its help now.

"Rowlet, please wake up!" you ask.

It opens its eyes, looks around, and sees you're stranded. It stands up ready to come to your rescue. You explain the situation.

"I need you to catch up with Ride Sharpedo and signal it to pick me up," you say. "I don't want Professor Kukui to know I made a mistake."

Rowlet flies over to Sharpedo.

"Rrrrr! Rrrrr!" Rowlet yelps, chasing after the speedy Pokémon.

But Sharpedo doesn't see or hear Rowlet. It's swimming so fast, it isn't taking the time to look up at the sky. Rowlet decides to tap it with its beak.

"Rrrrr!" Rowlet says, nudging Sharpedo.

"Sharrrrrpedo!" it replies with a snarl mistaking its tap for Peck.

Sharpedo jumps into the air and drops its jaw, showing its mouth full of fangs. It snaps at Rowlet. Luckily, Rowlet swerves just in time to dodge its Bite.

"Oh no!" you cry out, watching the scene unfold. "Rowlet, come back!"

Continue below.

GYARADOS:
Atrocious Pokémon

HEIGHT	21'04"
WEIGHT	518.1 lbs
TYPE	Water-Flying

Rowlet is flying as fast as it can. Sharpedo is right on its tail, trying to sink a bite in the Grass Quill Pokémon. Rowlet is flapping its wings as hard as it can, but it's starting to look tired.

"Hang in their Rowlet!" you say. "Fly as high as possible so Sharpedo can't reach you."

Help is on the way! You spot Professor Kukui riding a jet ski.

Vrrrrrrrooooooom! Professor Kukui's ride roars. It's loud enough to shoo Sharpedo away.

"Quick, hop on!" Professor Kukui says, steering back to safety on the shore.

"I'm so sorry for all the trouble, Professor Kukui," you say.

"I was so worried when I couldn't find you on the beach. How did you get all the way out there?" he asks.

"I just wanted to find a fossil to show you I'd be a great student," you explain, showing him the slab you found.

"Wow, that's an awesome fossil! It looks like it could be from Gyarados, the Atrocious Pokémon," Professor Kukui says. "But safety is more important than a fossil. When we explore Alola, we always do it together. Do you know why?"

You shake your head.

"Because it's more fun!" says Professor Kukui. "And so we can look out for each other."

"That makes sense," you say. "I'm looking forward to making friends at school to go on adventures with!"

"Well, you already have one," Professor Kukui says. "Me."

THE END

You try to take the shovel from the sand, but suddenly the mound grows. It opens its eyes and mouth. You take out your Pokédex and discover it's not a shovel but the Sand Heap Pokémon, Sandygast.

"I'm so sorry, I didn't realize…" you say, trying to apologize.

"Sss-sss-sandygaaaaaast!" it screams.

"Uh oh," you mutter.

Sandygast uses Sand Attack to throw sand in your face. You're going to need backup.

SANDYGAST:
Sand Heap Pokémon

HEIGHT	1'08"
WEIGHT	154.3 lbs
TYPE	Ghost-Ground

To use Alolan Raichu to battle it, continue below.

To battle with Rowlet, go to **PAGE 26**.

"Raichu, I choose you!" you say, tossing your Poké Ball.

Raichu arrives on the beach ready for battle!

"Use Thunderbolt, fast!" you ask.

"Rrrrrrrrrrrrrrrracihuuuuuu!" Raichu yelps.

The bolt surprises Sandygast. Maybe you should toss your Poké Ball and see if you can catch Sandygast?

To catch Sandygast, go to **PAGE 27**.

Or, to make your escape from the Sand Heap Pokémon, go to **PAGE 28**.

You toss your Poké Ball and Rowlet arrives. But since it's bright daylight, Rowlet is asleep.

"Rowlet, I need your help," you ask.

It wakes up and sees Sandygast.

"Rrrrrrr!" Rowlet says, taking to the sky.

And it's up in the air not a moment too soon because Sandygast hurls another Sand Attack. Rowlet dodges it with a swift swoop. Suddenly, you feel a rumbling underneath your feet.

"Uh oh. Let's get out of here!" you say.

You race across the beach as fast as possible with Rowlet above you. When you turn around, you see the sand shoot into the air with Sandygast's Earth Power.

You return Rowlet and find a new place to dig for a fossil. This time, you'll just use your hands. You dig and, eventually, you find a fossil!

"Awesome!" you cheer running your fingertips over a marking that looks like a feather.

You show your findings to Professor Kukui, who is still busy digging.

"This is a really cool Plume fossil!" Professor Kukui says. "This will be perfect for my lesson."

Now that you're done with your assignment, Professor Kukui suggests you go for a swim in the ocean.

"Race you to the water!" you say.

THE END

You toss your Poké Ball to Sandygast. It flashes in the sand.

Bing! You caught the Sand Heap Pokémon!

"All right!" you cheer. "I couldn't have done it without your help, Raichu."

"Raiiichu," it says, happy to have another Pokémon pal.

You can't wait to tell Professor Kukui!

"That's awesome!" Professor Kukui says.

"Now, Raichu and I are ready to keep looking for a fossil," you reply.

"No need, I already found one," Professor Kukui says.

"Cool! Can I see it?" you ask.

"Sure," Professor Kukui says with a smile. "When I see you in class tomorrow."

THE END

ALOLAN RAICHU:
Mouse Pokémon

HEIGHT	1'04"
WEIGHT	43.9 lbs
TYPE	Normal

"Rai-chu, rai-chu," Raichu chants while shoveling sand with its tail.

You're right by its side, digging with your hands.

"Raichu!" it says excitedly.

You look over and see something in the sand. It looks like some kind of old wood with markings on it.

"I can't wait to show this to Professor Kukui!" you tell Raichu.

You head over to show the Professor. He inspects the surface.

"Wow, it looks like you have a fossilized log that belonged to Komala. You can see its paw prints here," Professor Kukui explains. "Principal Oak will be so impressed by this find!"

"I couldn't have done it without my pal Raichu," you reply.

You can't wait to bring your fossil and your friend to school tomorrow!

THE END

You toss your Poké Ball and Beldum arrives on the beach. It hovers just above the sand.

"Beldum!" it greets you.

BELDUM:
Iron Ball Pokémon

HEIGHT	2'00"
WEIGHT	209.9 lbs
TYPE	Steel-Psychic

To guide Beldum along the shoreline to see what's washed up, continue below.

To see what could be buried by the beach's rocky cliffs, proceed to **PAGE 39**.

You lead Beldum along the water on a stroll. The tide rushes up and over your toes.

"Bel-bel-bel-bel!" Beldum beeps.

Beldum is using its magnetic power to sense what could be hidden in the sand. You are searching too, but with your eyes. Your thoughts are interrupted by your buddy.

"Beldum!" it signals you.

You kneel down in the sand and begin to dig in the exact spot Beldum showed you.

"Wow!" you say, pulling a metal statue from the sand.

TAPU KOKO:
Land Spirit Pokémon

HEIGHT	5'11"
WEIGHT	45.2 lbs
TYPE	Electric-Fairy

It looks brown with age, but you can still make out some of the painted markings.

"This must be ancient," you decide as you inspect it.

It seems to be the shape of an important Pokémon—Tapu Koko, the Island Guardian. Could it be a lost statue from a shrine to Tapu Koko?

Perhaps it washed up from an ancient shipwreck? Maybe it is Alolan treasure? This could be such a valuable find. Maybe it could wind up in museum!

You can't wait to show this statue to Professor Kukui!

Proceed below.

"Look what I found, Professor Kukui!" you say, presenting the statue.

Professor Kukui carefully examines it.

As he looks it over you add, "I think it's an ancient statue of the Island Guardian of Melemele, Tapu Koko. I wonder if it's from a shrine or a shipwreck?"

"You're right, it's Tapu Koko. And I can tell you where it comes from," Professor Kukui replies.

You are so excited! You can't wait to hear more.

"You can pick these up at the local market. They're a popular gift for tourists who visit the island," he says. "I have all four—Tapu Koko, Tapu Lele, Tapu Bulu, and Tapu Fini."

When you flip the figure over, you see the remnants of a price tag. You sigh with disappointment.

"I'm sorry to burst your bubble," Professor Kukui says. "But there's still plenty of time to keep searching. I know we'll find something if we don't give up!"

He's right. If at first you don't succeed, try, try again.

To keep looking with Beldum, go to **PAGE 32**.
To help Professor Kukui, go to **PAGE 33**.

Escavalier returns to the Pokémon Center lobby with its armor shined up. It's feeling much better now!

"Escavalier," it says, surprised to see you're still here.

You offer to lead Escavalier back to the beach, but it wants to continue the battle. It would like to have a thoughtful Trainer like you.

Escavalier is giving you another chance to catch it. You can't believe your luck!

Proceed to **PAGE 37**.

This time, you and Beldum will comb the sand away from the shoreline.

"Bel-bel-bel-bel," it beeps, using its magnetic force to scan.

Suddenly, Beldum gets pulled to a napping Pokémon.

"Escavalier!" it roars, angry to be awoken.

"Bellllllll!" Beldum shouts, scared.

Beldum has been drawn to the Cavalry Pokémon because its body is covered in steel armor.

"Esssssscavalier!" it belts with its lances in position, pointed straight at you. You try to apologize, but it is so unhappy to have its peace disturbed it immediately charges at you! The battle is clearly on.

ESCAVALIER:
Cavalry Pokémon

HEIGHT	3'03"
WEIGHT	72.8 lbs
TYPE	Bug-Steel

To have Beldum use Take Down, proceed to **PAGE 35**.

Or, to call on Mudbray, go to **PAGE 34**.

You check in with Professor Kukui.

"How's it going?" you ask.

"It's a nice day to be looking for a fossil," he says. "It'd also be nice to find one."

"That's why I'm here to help," you reply.

WISHIWASHI:
Small Fry Pokémon

HEIGHT	0'08"
WEIGHT	0.7 lbs
TYPE	Water

Professor Kukui explains that this beach is known for fossils. He hasn't had an easy time digging because the tide has been high so the sand is practically mud.

"I have an idea!" you announce. "Maybe my pal Mudbray can help."

You toss your Poké Ball and Mudbray arrives. You ask your Pokémon pal to uses its hooves to help Professor Kukui dig. Once it gets its hooves going, it clears the site in no time.

"Way to go, Mudbray!" you cheer it on.

Suddenly, Mudbray can't seem to dig any deeper. Professor Kukui examines the area and sees a large slab of stone. He starts to dust it off with a tiny broom.

"Wow, this looks like a fossil of Wishiwashi. It could be more than one." Professor Kukui says. "I can't thank you and Mudbray enough for your help."

"I can't wait to be there for that class," you reply.

"Well, it all starts tomorrow! See you back at school," Professor Kukui says.

THE END

"Mudbray, I need your help!" you ask, tossing your Poké Ball.

Mudbray gains strength and speed in wet sand, so you're hoping that will help in the battle with Escavalier. As it lands on the sand, you can't wait to set your strategy in motion.

But Escavalier is already in motion. In fact, it is charging right at you!

"Mudbray, use Mud-Slap," you begin.

Mudbray quickly hurls wet sand at Escavalier. Its aim is spot on and the Cavalry Pokémon finds itself covered in mud. It stops in mid-air and tries to move its armor, but its steel suit is jammed.

"Escavalieeeer," Escavalier says with surprise as it struggles to move its lances.

MUDBRAY:
Donkey Pokémon

HEIGHT	3'03"
WEIGHT	242.5 lbs
TYPE	Ground

While it's stuck, you decide this might be the perfect time to try to catch Escavalier. So, you toss your Poké Ball. It rolls and flashes in the sand, but Escavalier is soon ejected. Your strategy, while smart, has not made it weak enough to catch.

To keep battling, go to **PAGE 38**.

To take Escavalier to the Pokémon Center to clean up the mud, go to **PAGE 36**.

"Beldum, use Take Down!" you ask.

"Bellllllduuuuuuum!" it yelps, charging straight at Escavalier.

Escavalier doesn't flinch. The moment Beldum is in the range of its lances, it strikes with Twineedle.

"Essssssss," it hisses jabbing Beldum with the first lance. "Cavalieeeeer!" it shouts, striking with the other.

Beldum is left unable to battle. Escavalier happily returns to its nap.

"Thank you for everything, Beldum," you say, returning it to its Poké Ball.

You decide to take your pal for a good rest at the Pokémon Center. After all, you have a big first day of school tomorrow!

THE END

You return Beldum and walk over to Professor Kukui. You tell him you're taking Escavalier to the Pokémon Center.

"That's a nice thing to do," Professor Kukui says. "I'm looking forward to having such a caring student in my class."

You say goodbye to your new teacher and lead the Cavalry Pokémon to the Pokémon Center. Nurse Joy and Comfey greet you.

"We'll have you cleaned up in no time!" Nurse Joy tells Escavalier.

"Esssssscavalier," it thanks her.

You decide to wait in the lobby for your new friend. You think it might need help getting back to the beach.

COMFEY:
Posy Picker Pokémon

HEIGHT	0'04"
WEIGHT	0.7 lbs
TYPE	Fairy

Proceed to **PAGE 31**.

36

"Essssscavalieeeeer!" it yelps, ready to battle.

"Rrrrrrrrr!" Rowlet replies.

Escavalier charges at Rowlet with its lances pointed.

"Quick, Rowlet, use Ominous Wind!" you ask.

Rowlet flaps its wings, creating a gust of wind so strong Escavalier is sent flying back.

Escavalier tries to distract Rowlet with an ear-searing Bug Buzz.

"Rrrrrrrrr," it cries, trying to muffle the noise.

While Rowlet squirms, Escavalier begins to charge at it with Headbutt.

At the last moment you suggest, "Fly straight up and dodge it!"

Rowlet follows your instructions and shoots straight up in the sky. It narrowly misses Escavalier's Attack.

While Rowlet is still up in the sky, you have it fire a round of Razor Leaf. You then ask it to swoop back down and surprise Escavalier with a Brave Bird nosedive.

"Esssssssss!" Escavalier hisses, taking a direct hit.

You decide it is time and toss your Poké Ball. It flashes in the grass.

Bing!

You have caught your new Pokémon pal, Escavalier!

"Hooray!" you cheer. "I couldn't have done it without you Rowlet."

You can't wait to start school tomorrow with your old friend Rowlet and your new one, Escavalier.

THE END

A brave battler and true believer in itself, Escavalier won't give up! It decides that even though its armor is stuck, it's stuck in a good position. Its lances are pointed straight at Mudbray and that is just where they'll stay. Escavalier begins to charge again.

"Dodge it, Mudbray!" you ask.

Mudbray takes off running, but it soon finds itself away from the wet mud by the shoreline and in the dunes. Its hooves sink into the hot, dry sand. Escavalier makes its move.

"Essssssssscavalier!" it shouts, slamming into Mudbray with Headbutt.

Between the dunes and the direct hit, Mudbray is left unable to continue. You return it to its Poké Ball.

"Thank you for your help, Mudbray," you say.

Escavalier returns to its nap. In the sun, it's sure the wet sand will bake and flake right off.

You decide to take your Pokémon pal Mudbray to see Nurse Joy for a rest before school tomorrow. So you say so long to Professor Kukui and tell him you'll see him in the morning!

THE END

You and Beldum make your way across the sand to the rocky cliffs. You want to figure out which area would be best to search—in the sand near the rocks or on top of the rocks. You have Beldum scan the area.

"Bel-bel-bel," it replies, hovering over the sand.

"What about here?" you ask, pointing to some rocks.

"Bel-bel-bel," it says.

It doesn't seem to have a favorite side. It's up to you.

To climb up on the rocks, go to **PAGE 41**.

To stay in the sand, continue below.

"Bel-bel-Beldum!" it says, signaling you.

You jump down and run your fingers through the sand. You feel a ring with some charms or something on it. Perhaps it's a treasure from a shrine? You grab it and lift it up, excited to see what it is. But it's not an ancient find, it looks like someone lost their keys.

"Is anyone missing their key chain?" you shout to the nearby beachgoers.

You don't get a response, but you feel a response from what you've found.

Zzzzzzzap!

That's no key chain, that's Klefki, the Key Ring Pokémon. And it has just buzzed you and Beldum with a powerful Psyshock.

"Oh no! Run for it!" you tell Beldum.

You both race as fast as possible across the beach. Klefki chases you, threatening another jolt. But luckily, you outrun it.

When you reach Professor Kukui, you tell him the whole story.

"Klefki strikes again!" he says with a knowing nod. "You're not the first person in Alola to mistake that Pokémon for a pair of lost keys."

Now Professor Kukui shocks you in a good way. He found a Skull Fossil! You can't wait to learn more about it when school starts, officially, tomorrow.

KLEFKI:
Key Ring Pokémon

HEIGHT	0'08"
WEIGHT	6.6 lbs
TYPE	Steel-Fairy

THE END

"Bel-bel-Beldum!" it alerts you.

"Maybe this time it won't be a can!" you hope.

You bend over to take a closer look.

"Ugh, another can," you sigh. "That has to be the hundredth can today!"

"Belllldum," it replies with a nod.

You can't believe how much trash is trapped in these rocks. You decide to stop looking for a fossil. Instead, you want to do something about this litter problem.

You head back to talk to Professor Kukui. You tell him all about the trash you found in the rocks.

"I know it might take a long time to clean up, but I can't just leave all this litter here," you say.

"Beldum!" it agrees.

"You might be new to Alola, but you sure have the spirit!" Professor Kukui replies. "Here, nothing is more important than respecting nature and keeping the harmony between people and Pokémon."

Professor Kukui is so impressed by your dedication to the environment. He offers to help you with your beach clean-up!

Continue to **PAGE 42**.

Professor Kukui knows someone who could really help—Alolan Muk! Forget regular junk food, Muk's diet is pure garbage.

"With the help of Alolan Muk, we could have this beach trash-free in no time!" Professor Kukui says.

"But where can we find one?" you ask.

"I known just the place!" he replies.

Professor Kukui leads you to the local Pokémon Center. There, Nurse Joy introduces you to her multi-colored rainbow friend, Muk Alola Form.

"Nice to meet you, Muk," you say. "We could really use your help at the beach. I hope you're hungry!"

Alolan Muk roars that its appetite is ready. You, Beldum, and Professor Kukui lead it back to the rocks along the shore.

Beldum scans the rocks to find the trash. Alolan Muk springs into action chowing down on the litter like it's an all-you-can-eat buffet. Soon, half of the cliff is completely clean.

"Beldum! Beldum! Beldum!" it repeats to get your attention.

"What is it, Beldum?" you ask, taking a closer look. "Hmmm, it's some sort of cool coin."

You pick it up and show it to Professor Kukui.

"Let me see," Professor Kukui says. "Amazing! This coin appears to be from an ancient shipwreck in Alola."

"Wow!" you reply. "Way to go, Beldum,"

"Keep the coin in a safe place," Professor Kukui says. "It would be great for show and tell at school tomorrow."

"I'm looking forward to starting class. But the mission for today is to finish cleaning this beach!" you reply.

Alolan Muk roars in agreement. Professor Kukui is so impressed by your commitment to learning and nature. He can't wait to have you as a student.

ALOLAN MUK:
Sludge Pokémon

HEIGHT	3'03"
WEIGHT	114.6 lbs
TYPE	Poison-Dark

THE END

It seems like there's plenty of fun to be had right here at school, especially since you have it all to yourself!

You scan the Pokémon School with your eyes. You see a group of connected, round buildings with big arches lining the outdoor halls. They are piled high, but not as high as the large green tree beside it.

Could it be the tallest tree in Alola? Maybe you'll find out in school.

You spot a tower with a big golden bell. There's a walking bridge between two of the buildings and an awesome looking slide going down the side of one. There's a dirt track for racing and running with a perfect patch of green grass in the middle.

You see three footbridges over a small river that runs through the school. But the amazing ocean that surrounds Alola is just steps away. Can you imagine leaving school and being at the beach in a few strides? The Pokémon School just might be the coolest school ever!

But what do you want to do? To race around the track, continue below.

To climb up the bell tower, go to **PAGE 55.**

You have so much energy! You feel like you could run a million miles. You line up on the track. You kneel down and place your hands on the ground. 3. 2. 1! You take off down the path. The wind is blowing through your hair and you can feel your heart racing, just like you!

As you round the first corner, you hear a buzz. Fuzzzz!

You stop running to listen. What was that weird zap?!

Professor Kukui comes running out.

"Did you just hear that?" he asks you.

"Hm, I wonder what it was? I'm going to find out," he vows.

"Can I help you?" you offer.

"Sure!" Professor Kukui replies.

Continue below.

You follow Professor Kukui to the mechanical room. It's a dark place filled with connecting cables, levers on the wall, and metal boxes on the floor. This is where all the electricity for the school is controlled. You hear a low, unusual hum.

"I wonder where that buzz is coming from? Keep your eyes peeled," Professor Kukui asks, leading the way with a flashlight.

"Charjabug. Char-ja-bug!" you hear.

You look over a giant generator and see a small, green rectangle with square blue eyes and two yellow spikes. You stay quiet so as not to alarm it and tap Professor Kukui. He turns and flashes the light to find where the noise is coming from.

"Of course!" Professor Kukui exclaims. "Charjabug is trying to recharge! But you can't do it here, buddy, because we need this electricity for the school."

"Charjabuuuug," it sighs.

CHARJABUG:
Battery Pokémon

HEIGHT	1'08"
WEIGHT	23.1 lbs
TYPE	Bug-Electric

To help Charjabug boost its energy, continue below.

To see if Charjabug has a Trainer nearby, go to **PAGE 47**.

"Raichu, we need your help!" you say, tossing your Poké Ball.

Alolan Raichu looks to you, ready for action.

"Charjabug could use some more energy. Do you think you could share some of yours with it?" you ask.

"Raiiiiiiiicccchuuuuuuu!" it yelps with a nod, sending a bolt of electricity right to Charjabug.

Charjabug is glowing with yellow electric light. It's so bright, you have to squint just to see it.

"Wow, that was a powerful charge!" Professor Kukui says.

Raichu smiles, happy to help a fellow Pokémon in need.

"Do you think you could restore the school's generator too? I think one zap ought to do it," Professor Kukui asks.

Raichu nods again. It takes a few steps back to the wall to get a running start. It races across the room. It jumps up into the air and taps the generator with its tail, releasing a giant zap.

"Buzzzzz," the generator hums as its energy level is restored.

"Thank you so much, Raichu!" Professor Kukui says. "I'm looking forward to having you both in class tomorrow. Speaking of which, I better get back to setting up my classroom."

You say goodbye and return Alolan Raichu to its Poké Ball. You are excited to start school with such a cool teacher! But it seems you're not the only one who is excited. As you head across the school, Charjabug leaps in front of you. It won't let you leave.

"Chaarrrrrrj!" it rallies.

"Do you want to battle, Charjabug?" you ask.

"Char char Charjabug!" it confirms.

To choose your Fire-type friend Litten, go to **PAGE 51**.

To call on your pal Popplio, proceed to **PAGE 53**.

You leave Professor Kukui in the mechanical room to keep an eye on things and head toward the yard. You scan the school grounds in search of another student.

You spot someone tall, wearing an orange tank top, sitting under a tree. Could that be Charjabug's Trainer? You jog over to find out.

As you get close, you realize she's asleep. Should you wake her up? You would want to be woken up if it was your Pokémon.

"Um," you start. "Hi!"

"Ah!" she shouts, startled as she opens her eyes.

"Sorry to scare you," you say. "I was just wondering if you possibly know Charjabug?"

"Charjabug!" she says, looking around panicked. "Yes! Where did it go? It was just here taking a nap with me."

You show her the way. As you walk she introduces herself. Her name is Jillian. When you open the door to the mechanical room, Charjabug jumps into her arms.

"Charjabuuuuug!" it says, happy to be reunited.

"It's so good to see you too, buddy!" Jillian says. "But, oof, I think I got a sunburn on my shoulders from sleeping in the sun."

Professor Kukui explains that Charjabug had tapped into the school's generator to recharge.

"I'm so sorry! We just got back from a big camping trip over the break and Charjabug must have felt drained. We were both resting, but I guess it needs more than a nap," Jillian apologizes. Then she says to Charjabug, "I'm going to take you to Nurse Joy so you can recharge."

She returns Charjabug to its Poké Ball. Before she heads out, you have one more thing you would like to offer to help her with.

"Hey, about that sunburn," you begin. "I bet we can find a Pyukumuku at the beach. It has a healing goo that will soothe your skin."

"That would be awesome! Thank you. I'm a new student and I just arrived in Alola. I've never seen Pyukumuku before," she tells you.

"I'm a new student too!" you reply. "But I know the beach is this way. Let's put on our swimsuits and go."

"Sounds like a plan!" she replies.

PYUKUMUKU:
Sea Cucumber Pokémon

HEIGHT	1'00"
WEIGHT	2.6 lbs
TYPE	Water

Continue below.

You lead Jillian to the shore. You put on your snorkeling masks and head into the water.

As you paddle around the Alolan ocean, you spot some amazing Pokémon. There is Magikarp with its yellow whiskers. A school of big-eyed Wishiwashi swims by. Then you see a pink Alomomola making a splash. Below on some rocks, you spot a black ball with hot pink spikes and a white star—it's Pyukumuku!

You signal to Jillian and dive down to the Sea Cucumber Pokémon. You politely pet Pyukumuku to get some of its soothing goop on your hands. It's so cool and sticky, even in the warm water! You swim back to the shore.

Jillian meets you on the beach. You hand her your handful of Pyukumuku's special slime. She rubs it into her sunburn.

"I feel better already!" she cheers. "Thank you so much for your help. You're a real pal."

You smile, knowing you made your first friend even before school officially starts! Something tells you, this is going to be a fun year, maybe even the best year ever.

ALOMOMOLA:
Caring Pokémon

HEIGHT	3'11"
WEIGHT	69.7 lbs
TYPE	Water

THE END

You and Charjabug step out into the schoolyard. You want the sparks to fly on the field, not in the electrical wiring for the school.

"Litten, I choose you!" you say, tossing its Poké Ball into the air.

"Rrrrrawr!" Litten growls.

"Chaaaarrrjabug!" it replies.

You decide to make the first move.

"Litten, let's get started with Ember!" you order.

Charjabug dodges the Fire Cat Pokémon's series of small flames with Dig. It crawls into the ground. Litten runs over to the hole, hoping to fire an attack into it. But before it gets the chance, Charjabug pops up and surprises it with a Bug Bite chomp. Litten howls.

"Litten, are you okay?" you ask with concern.

"Rrrrrawr!" it says, ready to keep battling.

LITTEN:
Fire Cat Pokémon

HEIGHT	1'04"
WEIGHT	9.5 lbs
TYPE	Fire

To have Litten use Fury Swipes, proceed to the top of **PAGE 52**.

To try Flare Blitz from afar, turn to the bottom of **PAGE 52**.

While Charjabug is close, you think fast and have Litten use Fury Swipes.

"Rrrraaaaawr!" Litten growls, trying to claw Charjabug.

But the Battery Pokémon's boxy body barely feels a thing. It seizes the moment and ties up Litten with sticky String Shot.

Litten tries to bite itself out of the binds. While it's trapped, Charjabug ends the match with a zap.

"Chaaaaarjabug!" it yelps, chucking an electric charge with Spark.

Litten is left unable to battle. You return your Pokémon pal to its Poké Ball.

"Thank you, Litten, you were awesome out there," you say.

You then thank your new buddy Charjabug for the battle. You hope you'll see it around again when school starts… just not in the mechanical room.

THE END

Litten has scurried back to avoid another Bite. It looks up at you, awaiting instruction. You have a plan and its time to put it into action.

"Litten, use Flare Blitz!" you ask.

Litten turns into a fireball and flies over to Charjabug. The attack comes out so hot and fast, Charjabug barely knows what hit it.

"Now Litten, use Double Kick!" you instruct.

Litten wallops Charjabug with two legs for twice the punch.

Charjabug is looking pretty tired, so you figure it is time to toss your Poké Ball.

"Here's hoping you get to join me on my journey, Charjabug," you say as the Poké Ball flashes.

Bing!

You just caught your new Pokémon buddy, Charjabug! You give Litten a big hug.

"I couldn't have done it without you, pal," you tell Litten.

The day before school has been so exciting, you can't wait to see what more is in store when it's actually in session! You're so thrilled to be starting your first day with a new Pokémon friend, too. What more could you ask for?

THE END

"Popplio, I choose you!" you say, calling on your friend.

"Pop pop Popplio!" it says, happy to see you.

It's ready to battle and so is Charjabug. Will the bold Battery Pokémon make the first move?

POPPLIO:
Sea Lion Pokémon

HEIGHT	1'04"
WEIGHT	16.5 lbs
TYPE	Water

You don't waste a second before starting.

It's ready to battle and so is Charjabug. Will the bold Battery Pokémon make the first move? You don't waste a second before starting.

"Popplio, use Hydro Pump!" you instruct.

The Sea Lion Pokémon blasts a strong stream of water. But it is met in midair by Charjabug's fierce Thunderbolt! You both struck hard and fast and tried to be first. But this tie isn't working in your favor. In fact, it's backfiring.

Charjabug's terrific Thunderbolt has gone from powerful to unstoppable! Charjabug's Electric-type attack is made even stronger by Hydro Pump because water carries its electric current. Popplio just can't fight that intense charge, even if it did help make it so mighty!

You return Popplio to its Poké Ball.

"Thank you Popplio!" you say. "Now it's time to take you for a good rest at the Pokémon Center."

Like a good sport, you also thank Charjabug for the battle. You say goodbye and hurry off to see Nurse Joy as soon as possible. After all, tomorrow is a big day—your first day of school!

"Chaaarrrjabug!" Charjabug says goodbye.

You hope your paths cross again at school. And hopefully, when they do, they'll be time for a rematch!

THE END

You lost count of the number of steps you've climbed to get to the top of the school building. You start to count backwards as you race up the last few. 10, 9, 8, 7, 6, 5, 4, 3, 2, 1... You've arrived! You'd cheer, but you're too out of breath. As you huff and puff, you get a good look at the big, golden bell. Perhaps someday, you'll get to ring it.

For now, you're going to enjoy your view of the entire school. It's beautiful up here. The breeze blows through your hair and brings the salty scent of the sea nearby.

You look down and see your new teacher walking toward the arch at the entrance. Professor Kukui's carrying a ladder. He must be working on a project. Maybe you could go sneak in and poke around your new classroom, since you know Professor Kukui will be gone for a while?

If you want to take a peek while no one is there, go to **PAGE 56**.
Or, to help Professor Kukui, go to **PAGE 60**.

You walk down the round hallway reading the signs on each door. You're looking for your classroom. There it is!

You walk through the open archway and into Professor Kukui's room. The far wall is lined with books. There is a ladder that runs to the ceiling. Colorful charts and pictures of Pokémon dot the green walls. There are five half-circle desks with wooden chairs facing the blackboard. You wonder which desk is yours?

You start to walk to see what else you can find out. The lights flicker.

"What was that?!" you gasp.

Is someone there? But you look at the light switch on the wall and you don't see anyone.

The lights flicker again. You scream. But no one comes.

To leave the classroom and tell Professor Kukui, continue below.

To take out Rowlet, proceed to **PAGE 58**.

You sprint down the steps of the school and run across the yard. Professor Kukui is up on the ladder at the arch. He puts his rag down and stops what he's doing when you approach.

"Are you okay?" he wonders. "You look like you've seen a Ghost-type!"

You admit to your teacher that you were sneaking around the classroom.

"That's no big deal. Tomorrow it will be your classroom, too!" he replies. "Is that why you're so panicked?"

"Well, while I was there, the lights flickered. Twice," you explain. "But I didn't see anyone."

"That must have been weird," Professor Kukui laughs. "Don't worry, our Principal, Samson Oak, has a maintenance crew visiting today. They must have been testing the power lines."

You breathe a deep sigh of relief! You offer to help Kukui shine up the sign. He tosses you a spare rag. You dip it in the bucket of soapy water and you wipe down the sides of the arch.

When you're both done, Professor Kukui thanks you for your help. And he has an awesome idea!

"Before you go, do you want to race around the track on the Ride Tauros?" Professor Kukui offers.

"Yes!" you exclaim.

He tells you to wait at the track. You can hardly contain your excitement.

Professor Kukui soon returns with Tauros. It has two sharp grey horns and three tails. On its back is a saddle.

"Here, let me help you hop on," Professor Kukui says, offering you a hand.

You jump up onto its back. Before you can say Wild Bull Pokémon, you're off! Tauros gallops around the track so fast you can barely keep your grip on the saddle.

"Yippee!" you yell.

Tauros roars back in agreement. After a single lap you know why the people and Pokémon of Alola love to ride together. It's so much fun!

But tomorrow is a big day, so you say goodbye to your new pal Tauros and your new teacher, Professor Kukui.

"I'm looking forward to seeing you tomorrow!" Professor Kukui says.

"Me too," you reply.

THE END

"Rowlet, I need your help!" you say, tossing its Poké Ball in the air.

Rowlet arrives, but is in a deep sleep because it's daytime. During the day it builds up energy and then its up all night. But you need Rowlet right now!

"Roooowwwlet!" you say, gently tapping your friend.

It opens one eye. You smile back at it. It closes its eye again. It wants to sleep.

Then suddenly a floating black ball with big fangs and even bigger eyes appears before you.

"Gassssss!" it hisses.

"Rrrrrrrr!" Rowlet screams.

Rowlet races to your side, scared. You take out your Pokédex to figure out exactly what you're facing. Before you can read a word, it hurls a blob of deep, dark smoke at you.

"It's Shadow Ball!" you warn. "Run!"

You and Rowlet speed right out of class. You run so fast you don't realize you've run right into Principal Samson Oak.

"You look like you're feeling Gastly!" Principal Samson Oak says doing a spot-on impression of the Pokémon they just ran from.

"Principal Oak!" you exclaim. "We just saw a scary Pokémon, it looked like a black ball with sharp teeth! And it spit smoke at us!

"Yep, that's Gastly," Principal Oak confirms. "A wild Gastly has been spotted on school grounds. You're not the first student it has scared. My guess is in time, just like gas, it will pass."

You heart is racing, but you laugh at his joke.

"Okay, Rowlet, I guess we better get going. That was enough excitement for one day," you say.

GASTLY:
Gas Pokémon

HEIGHT	4'03"
WEIGHT	0.2 lbs
TYPE	Ghost-Poison

"Well, just wait until school starts tomorrow! That's when the real fun begins," Principal Oak promises, continuing his march down the hallway.

"Rrrrr!" Rowlet cheers, ready for tomorrow.

THE END

You walk across campus to Professor Kukui. You say hi to your new teacher and introduce yourself.

"Looking forward to having you in class tomorrow!" he says.

"I'm so excited to start school, I accidentally came a day early!" you admit with a smile. "Since I'm here, would you like some help?"

"Sure!" Professor Kukui says. "I want to secure this welcome sign and some streamers to this arch."

"I bet my pal Rowlet could help!" you offer.

You toss you Poké Ball and cross your fingers that Rowlet will wake up. It typically likes to be up at night and sleep during the day. But with an important person like Professor Kukui before it, Rowlet opens its eyes and is ready to help!

"Rowlet, can you take the end of the blue streamer and fly it up to me?" Professor Kukui asks.

"Rrrrrr!" it replies, springing into action.

"Thank you!" Professor Kukui says.

Soon you have a rhythm going. You twirl the streamers, Rowlet flies them to Professor Kukui, and then the Professor tapes them to the arch. In no time, the decorations are done. And, if you do say so yourself, they look awesome.

"With your help, we finished ahead of schedule. Now I have a free afternoon," Professor Kukui says. "Want to hit to the beach?"

"You bet!" you cheer.

"Rrrrrr!" Rowlet agrees.

To go fishing, continue below.

If you have a need for speed, proceed to **PAGE 63**.

Alola has some of the most beautiful beaches in the world. The sea is filled with an amazing array of Pokémon. Water-types truly thrive in the crystal blue water and you set your hopes on catching one!

You follow Professor Kukui to the edge of the sand. You climb onto some smooth, grey rock slabs. They are warm beneath your feet from baking in the sun all day.

"I think this will be the perfect spot," Professor Kukui says, handing you a fishing rod.

You cast a line out into the water. There is nothing to do but shoot the breeze and stare off into the sea, sparkling in the sunshine. Alola is so peaceful.

Your peace is soon disturbed because you feel something tugging on your line.

"All right!" you say, reeling in your catch.

Suddenly, a bold and brightly patterned Bruxish bursts through the water.

"Wow!" you say, quickly taking it off the line and putting it in a bucket filled with salt water. "I hope I can catch you for good, Bruxish."

"Only one way to find out," Professor Kukui reminds you.

You toss your Poké Ball and become Bruxish's new buddy! You can't wait to train together.

You thank Professor Kukui for taking you fishing. What a fun day it turned out to be! You can only imagine how great each day of school will be with a teacher like Professor Kukui. Well, looks like you'll get to find out tomorrow...and you can't wait!

BRUXISH:
Gnash Teeth Pokémon

HEIGHT	2'11"
WEIGHT	41.9 lbs
TYPE	Water-Psychic

THE END